The History of Telephones

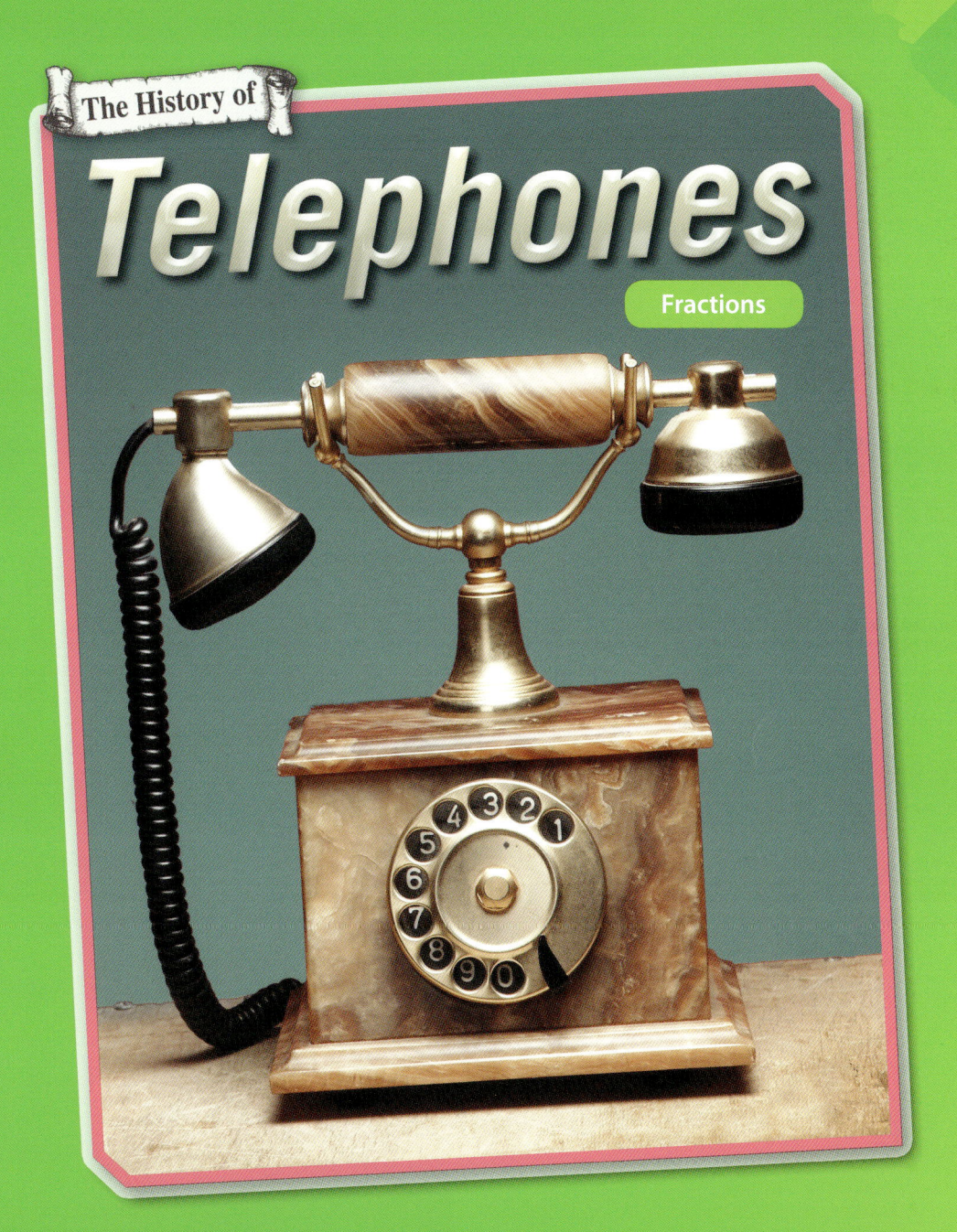

Fractions

Kristy Stark, M.A.Ed.

Consultants

Michele Ogden, Ed.D
Principal
Irvine Unified School District

Colleen Pollitt, M.A.Ed.
Math Support Teacher
Howard County Public Schools

Publishing Credits

Rachelle Cracchiolo, M.S.Ed., *Publisher*
Conni Medina, M.A.Ed., *Managing Editor*
Dona Herweck Rice, *Series Developer*
Emily R. Smith, M.A.Ed., *Series Developer*
Diana Kenney, M.A.Ed., NBCT, *Content Director*
Stacy Monsman, M.A., *Editor*
Kevin Panter, *Graphic Designer*

Image Credits: p.9 Album/Oronoz/Newscom; p.10 Photo Researchers, Inc./Alamy Stock Photo; pp.10–11 World History Archive/Newscom; p.13 Pictorial Press Ltd/Alamy Stock Photo; pp.15 (top), 27 (upper left corner) Creative Commons Attribution 3.0 Unported by CTG Publishing www.ctgpublishing.com; p.15 (full page) Fox Photos/Getty Images; p.17 Jonathan Kirn/Corbis via Getty Images; p.18 Bettmann/Getty Images; p.19 SSPL/Getty Images; p.20 Chris Willson/Alamy Stock Photo; p.21 Eloy Alonso/Reuters; p.22 David Paul Morris/Getty Images; pp.23, 24, 27 (upper right corner) Vivek Prakash/Reuters; p.25 NASA; p.27 (center) Stefan Sollfors/Alamy Stock Photo, (lower left corner) Jack Sullivan/Alamy Stock Photo, (second from bottom right corner) Chris Willson/Alamy Stock Photo; all other images from iStock and/or Shutterstock.

Library of Congress Cataloging-in-Publication Data

Names: Stark, Kristy, author.
Title: The history of telephones / Kristy Stark, M.A.Ed.
Description: Huntington Beach, CA : Teacher Created Materials, Inc, [2018] | Audience: Grade 4 to 6. | Includes index.
Identifiers: LCCN 2017012135 (print) | LCCN 2017037243 (ebook) | ISBN 9781480759381 (eBook) | ISBN 9781425855567 (pbk.)
Subjects: LCSH: Telephone--History--Juvenile literature.
Classification: LCC TK6165 (ebook) | LCC TK6165 .S73 2018 (print) | DDC 621.386--dc23
LC record available at https://lccn.loc.gov/2017012135

Teacher Created Materials

5301 Oceanus Drive
Huntington Beach, CA 92649-1030
http://www.tcmpub.com

ISBN 978-1-4258-5556-7
© 2018 Teacher Created Materials, Inc

Table of Contents

Traveling Back in Time 4

Meeting Mr. Bell and Mr. Watson 8

Changing Phone Designs 14

Exploring the 1960s and 1970s 18

Phones Get Smarter 22

Returning Home 26

Problem Solving 28

Glossary 30

Index 31

Answer Key 32

   This is a work of fiction. Characters, businesses, events, and incidents are either the products of the author's imagination or used in a fictitious manner. Any resemblance to actual persons, living or dead, or actual events is purely coincidental.

Traveling Back in Time

It is getting late, and the sun is about to set. Bryce hopes he can use the last bit of daylight to finish his work. The old telephone booth is a great find from the junkyard. It is the perfect **contraption** for making a time machine.

Bryce has been working on his time machine for several months. His scientist parents built their own time machines when they were about his age. They helped him when he needed it, but he was able to do most of the work on his own.

As the sun begins to set, Bryce tightens the final screw on the machine's control panel. "There, that should do it," he says. The only thing left to do is test the machine.

Bryce sits on the seat he bolted to the inside of the telephone booth and buckles his seat belt. Then, he thinks about where he should travel first.

LET'S EXPLORE MATH

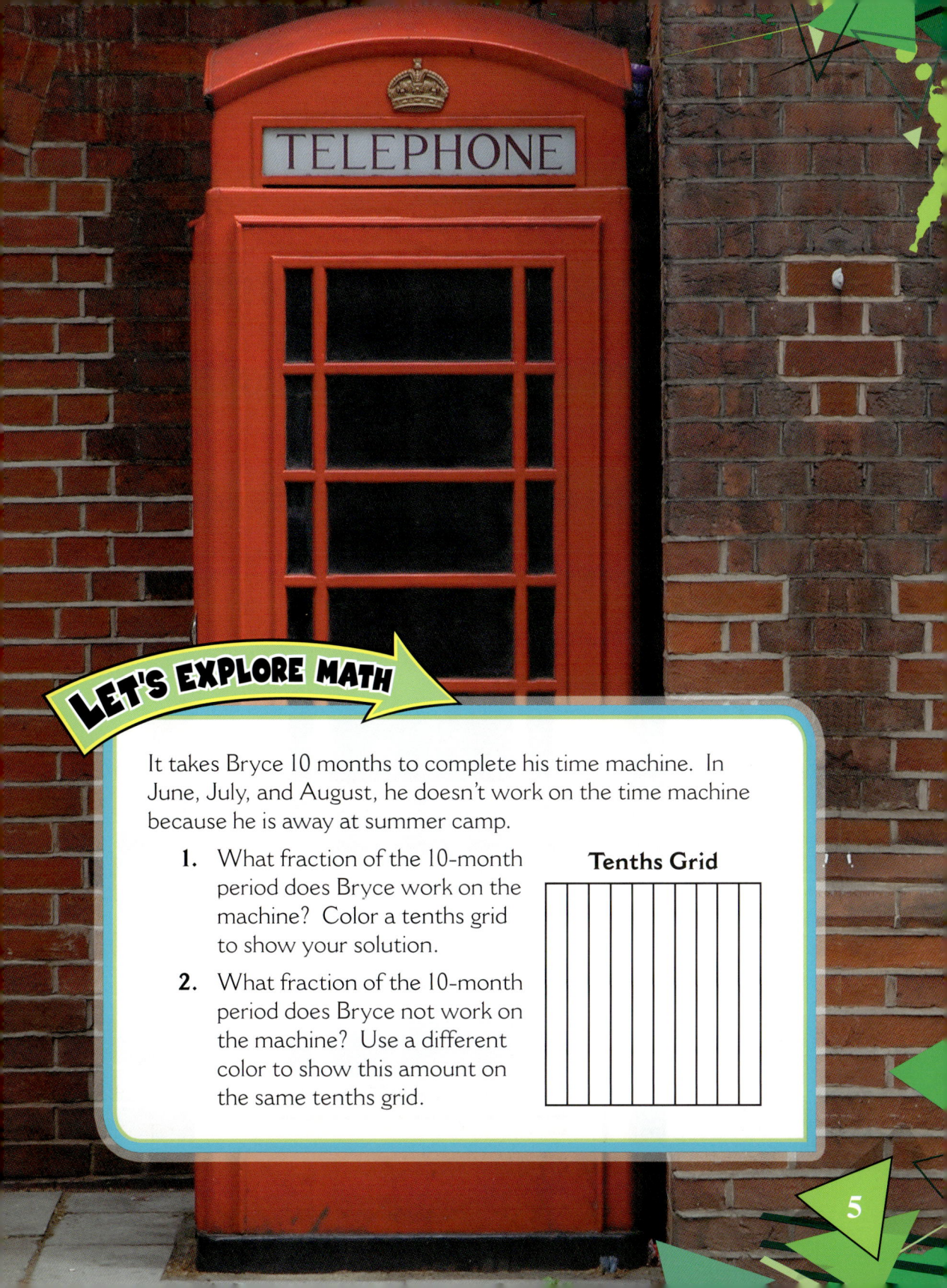

It takes Bryce 10 months to complete his time machine. In June, July, and August, he doesn't work on the time machine because he is away at summer camp.

1. What fraction of the 10-month period does Bryce work on the machine? Color a tenths grid to show your solution.

2. What fraction of the 10-month period does Bryce not work on the machine? Use a different color to show this amount on the same tenths grid.

Tenths Grid

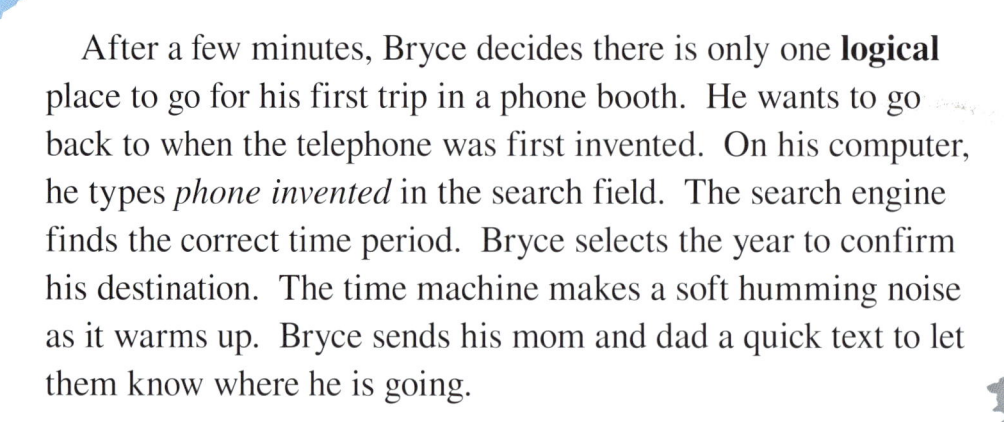

After a few minutes, Bryce decides there is only one **logical** place to go for his first trip in a phone booth. He wants to go back to when the telephone was first invented. On his computer, he types *phone invented* in the search field. The search engine finds the correct time period. Bryce selects the year to confirm his destination. The time machine makes a soft humming noise as it warms up. Bryce sends his mom and dad a quick text to let them know where he is going.

At first, nothing happens. He looks down at the screen, confused. Suddenly, the booth starts to rattle and shake. There is a quick flash of light as his house disappears before his eyes. "Okay, 1876, here I come!" Bryce yells excitedly as he feels the phone booth fly through the air.

Meeting Mr. Bell and Mr. Watson

After a few seconds, the phone booth lands in a small room. There is a desk that is covered with tools and papers. Bryce sees a device with a wooden base. It's the first telephone!

Bryce unbuckles his seat belt. Then, he opens the phone booth's door slowly. He sees two men shaking hands. They look very happy. The men notice Bryce and say hello. They introduce themselves as Alexander Graham Bell and Thomas Watson. Bryce explains that he is from the future. He points to the device on the desk and asks, "Can you tell me about your invention?"

Bell tells Bryce that his idea is based on the electric telegraph, which was invented by Samuel Morse in the 1830s. The telegraph uses a code of long and short **pulses** to send messages through an **electric current**.

Bell (left) and Watson (right) discuss their invention in 1876.

LET'S EXPLORE MATH

Imagine that a telegraph uses 10 pulses to send a message. The message has 6 long pulses and 4 short pulses. The fraction of the message with long pulses is $\frac{6}{10}$.

1. Write an equivalent fraction for $\frac{6}{10}$ with a denominator of 100. Color a tenths grid and a hundredths grid to show this amount. $\frac{6}{10} = \frac{\Box}{100}$

Tenths Grid

Hundredths Grid

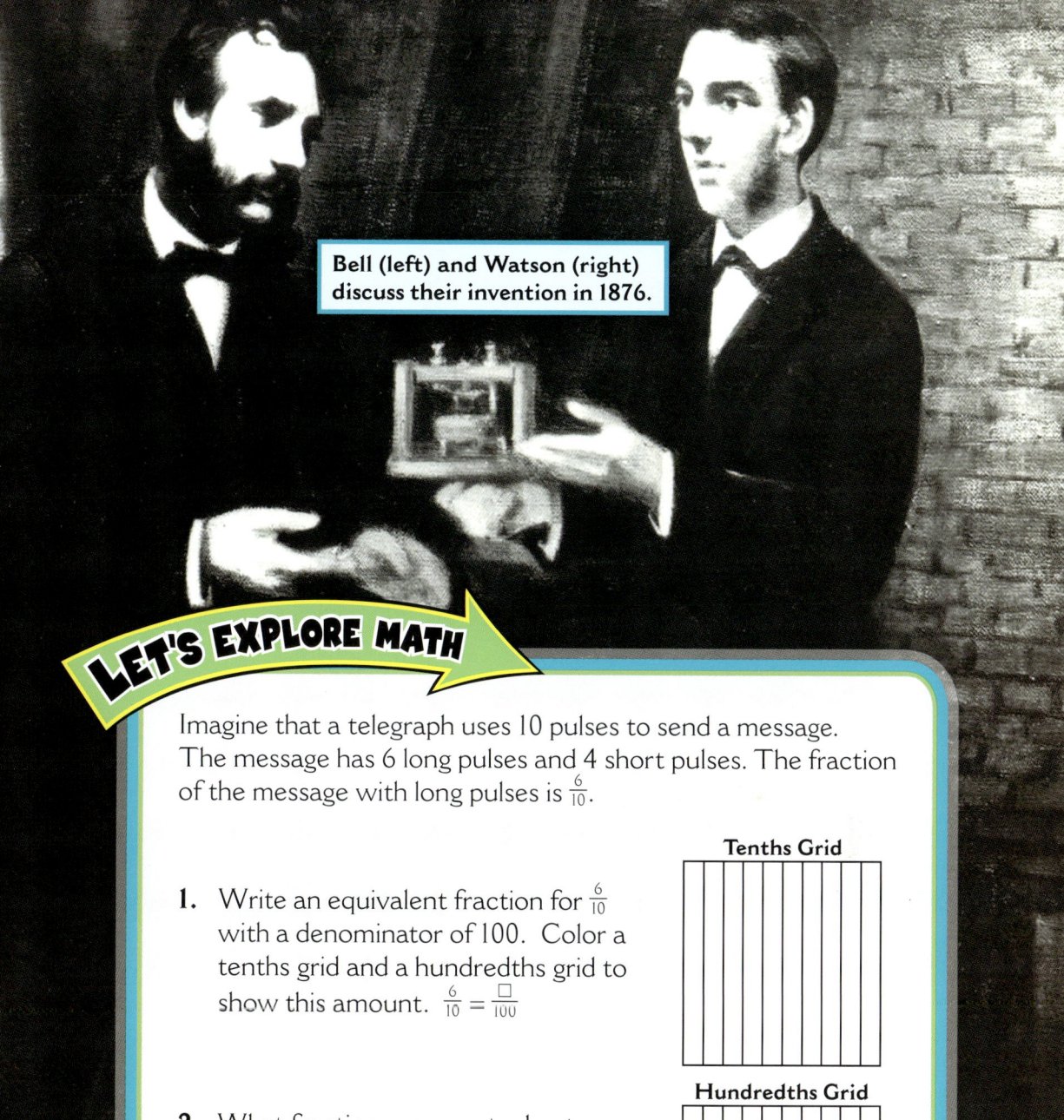

2. What fraction represents short pulses? Write this fraction in tenths and hundredths. Use a different color to show this amount on the same grids. $\frac{\Box}{10} = \frac{\Box}{100}$

9

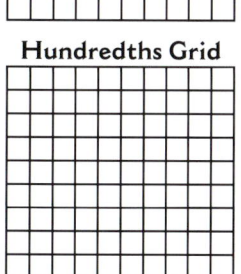

2 Sheets—Sheet 2.

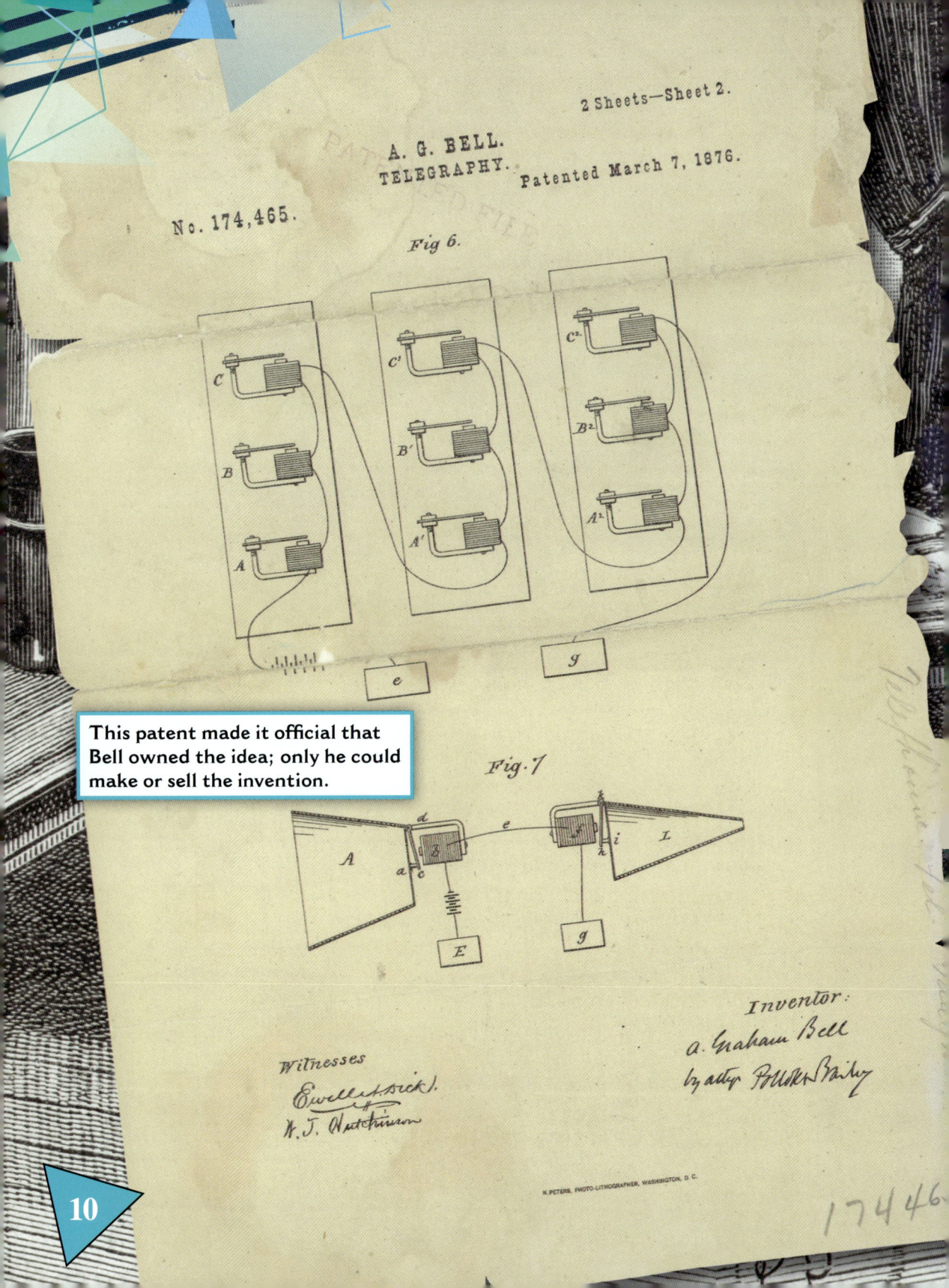

A. G. BELL.
TELEGRAPHY.

No. 174,465. Patented March 7, 1876.

Fig. 6.

This patent made it official that Bell owned the idea; only he could make or sell the invention.

Fig. 7.

Witnesses
Ewell Patrick
N. J. Hutchinson

Inventor:
A. Graham Bell
by atty Pollok & Bailey

10

Gray (right) files for a telephone patent on the same day as Bell (left).

Bell explains that he wanted to create a device that would use electricity to **transmit** speech.

"I am not an electrician. So, I hired Mr. Watson to help me," says Bell. "On March 7, 1876, I received a **patent** for our work. I found out that another man had been working on a telephone as well. Elisha Gray was making one at the exact same time. He even filed for a patent on the same day! What are the odds of that? Lucky for me, I was the one to get the patent for the telephone."

"Is that why you looked so happy when I got here?" asks Bryce.

Bell replies, "No, we were celebrating for a different reason. It has been three days since I received the patent. And today, Watson heard me speak through the telephone!"

Bryce is amazed. "What did you say to Mr. Watson?" he asks.

"I said, 'Mr. Watson, come here. I want to see you.' He was in another room and heard me through the telephone. Isn't that amazing? I believe this telephone is going to change the world as we know it. Do you think that someday everyone will have a telephone?"

"Your invention will definitely change everything, Mr. Bell. I know that everyone in the world will have a telephone. In a little over one hundred years, people will even have telephones that fit in their pockets."

Bell and Watson laugh as they pat each other on the back. "Telephones for everyone!" laughs Watson as he shakes his head.

"Thank you for your time, Mr. Bell and Mr. Watson. I need to get going. I have several more stops to make," says Bryce as he buckles his seat belt.

As the time machine warms up, Bryce wonders whether the men realize just how much their invention will impact future generations.

Watson hears Bell's voice through the telephone for the first time.

Changing Phone Designs

Bryce decides he wants to learn how phones changed after Bell's design. He travels from the 1880s to the early 1900s. He sees that phones changed greatly during this time. They look very different from Bell's original phone.

Bryce continues through time. He watches as people get phones for their homes and businesses. He sees a candlestick phone. In the 1890s, the first candlestick phones had two separate pieces. One piece was held up to the mouth. The other piece was held to the ear. This made it possible to listen to the person on the other end of the phone line. In the late 1920s, a new design connected the mouthpiece to the **receiver**.

Bryce also sees men building public phone booths. These booths are more **elegant** than Bryce's phone booth. The booths have rugs and lace curtains. They have fancy cabinets made of polished wood, too.

1876

1892

1927

15

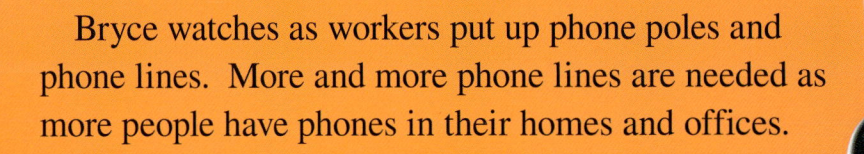

Bryce watches as workers put up phone poles and phone lines. More and more phone lines are needed as more people have phones in their homes and offices.

Bryce learns that by 1919, most people had rotary phones. These phones have circular dials with digits 0 through 9. People rotated the dial to a digit and then released it. People repeated this process for each digit of the phone number. Bryce dials his home phone number on the rotary phone. He is shocked by how long it takes to dial! *Thank goodness this phone was replaced*, Bryce thinks. *It takes way too long to make a call!*

Bryce wonders exactly when the rotary phone was replaced by push buttons. He types his **query** into the search field on his computer. He selects the time period. It doesn't take long before Bryce is on his way again!

rotary phone from the 1920s

A lineman works on a phone pole in 1920.

LET'S EXPLORE MATH

A dial on a rotary phone has 10 digits from 0 to 9. On the dial, $\frac{5}{10}$ of the digits are odd and $\frac{50}{100}$ of the digits are even. Color a tenths grid and a hundredths grid to show the fractions of odd and even digits on the rotary phone. Then, add the fractions by writing equivalent fractions.

Tenths Grid

Hundredths Grid

Touch-Tone telephone from 1963

Exploring the 1960s and 1970s

For his next stop, Bryce lands in 1963. He is at the headquarters of the American Telephone and Telegraph Company (AT&T). Bryce sees the Touch-Tone telephone. He learns that it was the first push-button phone on the market. The Touch-Tone is not like the rotary phone. This phone has a keypad to dial numbers. Each key has a unique **frequency**. Each frequency sends a signal to the operator to tell which digit was dialed.

Bryce sees another machine in the company's office. It does not look like anything he's ever seen. It has buttons and a light that blinks. It looks like a small box. Bryce learns that the box is an answering machine.

People used answering machines when they weren't able to answer their phones. Messages were recorded on **cassette tapes**. They were used by many people until the early 2000s.

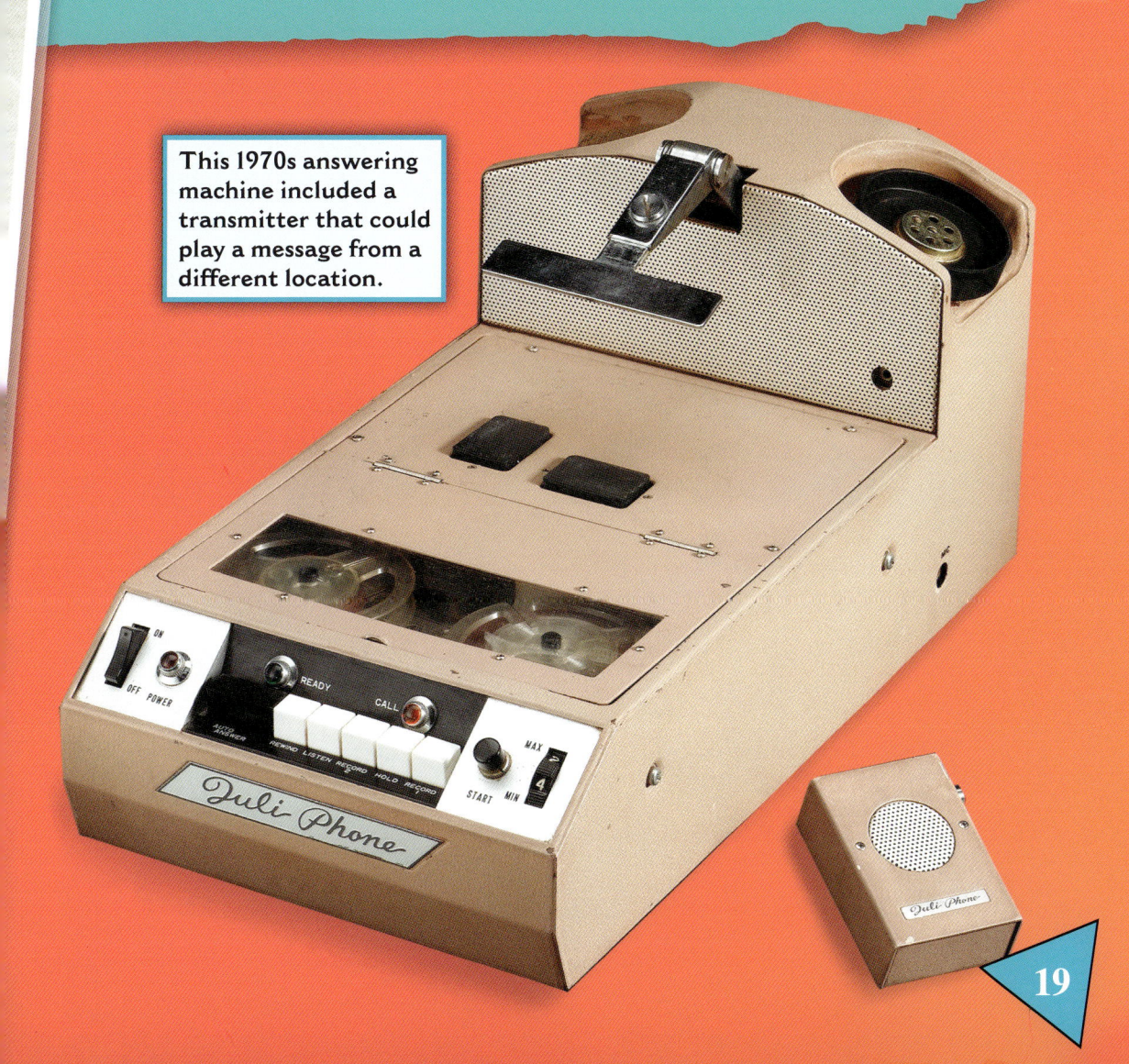

This 1970s answering machine included a transmitter that could play a message from a different location.

Bryce thinks about where he would like to go next. He decides to travel to see the invention of the first cell phone. He is surprised to learn that it was invented about 10 years after the first push-button phone.

Bryce lands in 1973. He meets Martin Cooper, an engineer. Cooper works for a company called Motorola. He tells Bryce that people want to be able to make phone calls at anytime and from anywhere. Cooper says, "I made my first phone call from a sidewalk in New York City. I called my rival, Joel Engel. He works for Bell Labs. I just wanted him to know that I beat him to the punch—I invented the first cellular phone!"

The first cell phone was sold about 10 years later, in 1984. But, more research needed to be done to perfect it. Not many people had one. It was very expensive. It cost about $4,000! Bryce learns that people could only talk for about 30 minutes at a time on these phones. Then, the phones had to be charged for 10 hours!

cellular phone from 1984

Cooper poses with his invention.

LET'S EXPLORE MATH

The first cell phone took 10 hours to charge. Imagine that Martin Cooper charged his phone for 4 hours in the morning and 6 hours in the evening.

1. Color a tenths circle to show the fraction of time that the phone charged in the morning. Color a hundredths circle to show the fraction of time that the phone charged in the evening.

2. What fraction represents the total amount of time Cooper charged his phone? Write the answer in tenths and hundredths.

Tenths Circle

Hundredths Circle

Steve Jobs introduces the iPhone® in San Francisco, California, in 2007.

Phones Get Smarter

Just as Bryce ponders what he would do if he had to wait 10 hours for his phone to charge, he gets a text from his mom. She wants him to head home soon. Dinner is almost ready. "One more stop," Bryce texts back.

Bryce knows that cell phones changed a lot after 1973. Phones were made smaller and had longer-lasting batteries. Games and cameras were added to phones, too. Bryce is starting to realize just how much the invention of the **smartphone** revolutionized the way people communicate. And that's exactly what he wants to see next!

The time machine takes Bryce to 2007. He is at Apple® headquarters. He sees Steve Jobs introducing the iPhone®. Jobs explains that this new phone does more than make calls and take pictures. It has a touch screen and works like a mini computer. The phone can browse the Internet, play music, use apps, and send texts.

Bryce, of course, knows all of this. But, he is grateful to witness this moment in history. Before now, he hadn't realized that the iPhone® was launched the same year he was born. *Wow, 2007 was an important year for so many reasons!* Bryce thinks.

LET'S EXPLORE MATH

Bryce asks 10 friends how they most frequently use their smartphones. He asks them to choose from the following categories: music, email, Internet browsing, and games. Bryce records their responses in the tenths circle shown below.

Smartphone Usage

- music
- Internet browsing
- email
- games

1. Write a fraction for each category of the tenths circle.
2. Rename each fraction in hundredths.
3. What fraction of students uses their smartphones for music and games? Write this fraction in tenths and hundredths.

first Android phone

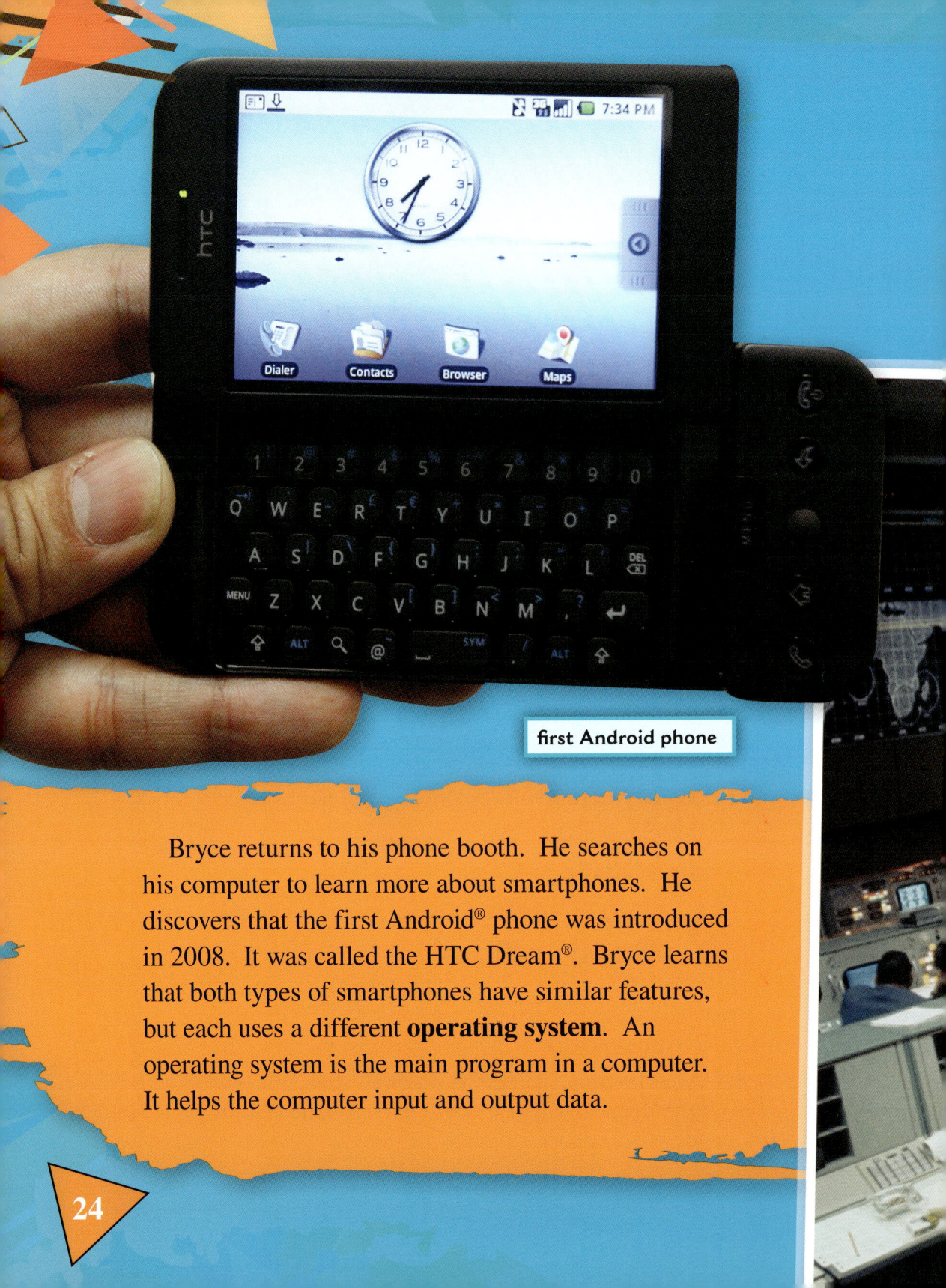

Bryce returns to his phone booth. He searches on his computer to learn more about smartphones. He discovers that the first Android® phone was introduced in 2008. It was called the HTC Dream®. Bryce learns that both types of smartphones have similar features, but each uses a different **operating system**. An operating system is the main program in a computer. It helps the computer input and output data.

Besides operating systems, the phones actually have one key thing in common. They both have computers inside! These computers are more powerful than the ones NASA used to send people to the moon in 1969. Bryce pulls his smartphone from his pocket. He stares at it. *No wonder my mom is always telling me to take good care of my phone.*

Bryce suddenly remembers his mom's text. He warms up the time machine. As he waits, he wonders how smartphones will change in the future. *Who knows,* thinks Bryce, *maybe I'll be the person who invents the next amazing phone.*

NASA mission control center in 1969

Returning Home

"Mom. Dad. I'm home," Bryce calls as he exits the phone booth.

"How was your trip?" his mom asks as she hugs him.

Bryce tells his parents about visiting Bell and Watson. He tells them about each invention he saw, from the candlestick phone to smartphones.

Bryce wants to remember this experience and what he learned. So, the next day, he creates a time line. It shows all the things he saw on his adventure. He includes important dates and people. He also draws a picture of each invention.

Bryce decides there are two very important people who need to see his time line. He places a copy of it in his time machine. He sends the time line to Bell and Watson with a note. *I thought you would like to see just how much your invention changes over time. Your friend, Bryce.*

1876

2008

1892

2007

1973

1937

1963

27

Problem Solving

Oak Elementary School is having a fundraiser to buy new P.E. equipment. They're asking people to turn in their old cell phones. The old phones will be recycled, and the school will get money in return.

The table on the right shows the fraction of students (per grade level) who collected cell phones.

1. Which grade level had the greatest fraction of students collect old cell phones? How do you know?

2. Which grade level had the least fraction of students collect old cell phones? How do you know?

3. What fraction of students collected cell phones in grades 1 and 2? Explain your thinking.

4. What fraction of students collected cell phones in grades 3 and 4? Explain your thinking.

5. Which two grades had the greatest fraction of students collect cell phones: grades 1 and 2, or grades 3 and 4? Explain your reasoning.

Fraction of Students Who Collected Cell Phones	
Grade Level	Students
1	$\frac{6}{10}$
2	$\frac{34}{100}$
3	$\frac{3}{10}$
4	$\frac{52}{100}$

29

Glossary

cassette tapes—small cases that contain magnetic tape to record or play back audio

contraption—a piece of unusual equipment

electric current—a flow of electricity

elegant—high quality

frequency—the number of times a sound wave or radio wave repeats per second

logical—reasonable

operating system—the main program in a computer

patent—an official document that gives a person the right to be the only one that makes or sells a product

pulses—brief increases in the amount of light, sound, or electricity

query—a question or request for information

receiver—the part of a telephone that is spoken into

smartphone—a cell phone that can send and receive emails and texts, browse the Internet, take photos, and more

transmit—to send signals

Index

American Telephone and Telegraph Company (AT&T), 18

Android, 24

Apple, 23

Bell, Alexander Graham, 8–14, 26

candlestick phone, 14, 26

cellular phone, 20

Cooper, Martin, 20–21

Engel, Joel, 20

Gray, Elisha, 11

iPhone, 22–23

Jobs, Steve, 22–23

Morse, Samuel, 8

Motorola, 20

patent, 10–11

rotary phones, 16, 18

smartphone, 22, 24–26

telegraph, 8

Touch-Tone, 18

Watson, Thomas, 8–9, 11–13, 26

Answer Key

Let's Explore Math

page 5:
1. $\frac{7}{10}$; 7 out of 10 parts in the tenths grid should be one color
2. $\frac{3}{10}$; 3 out of 10 parts in the tenths grid should be a different color

page 9:
1. $\frac{6}{10} = \frac{60}{100}$; 6 out of 10 parts of the tenths grid and 60 out of 100 parts in the hundredths grid should be one color
2. $\frac{4}{10} = \frac{40}{100}$; 4 out of 10 parts of the tenths grid and 40 out of 100 parts in the hundredths grid should be a different color

page 17:
Odd digits: $\frac{5}{10} = \frac{50}{100}$;
Even digits: $\frac{5}{10} = \frac{50}{100}$;
$\frac{5}{10} + \frac{5}{10} = \frac{10}{10}$ or 1; $\frac{50}{100} + \frac{50}{100} = \frac{100}{100}$ or 1; 10 out of 10 parts in the tenths grid and 100 out of 100 parts in the hundredths should be colored

page 21:
1. $\frac{4}{10}$; 4 out of 10 parts in the tenths circle should be colored; $\frac{60}{100}$; 60 out of 100 parts in the hundredths circle should be colored
2. $\frac{10}{10} = \frac{100}{100}$

page 23:
1. music: $\frac{2}{10}$
   email: $\frac{2}{10}$
   Internet browsing: $\frac{3}{10}$
   games: $\frac{3}{10}$
2. music: $\frac{2}{10} = \frac{20}{100}$
   email: $\frac{2}{10} = \frac{20}{100}$
   Internet browsing: $\frac{3}{10} = \frac{30}{100}$
   games: $\frac{3}{10} = \frac{30}{100}$
3. $\frac{2}{10} + \frac{3}{10} = \frac{5}{10}$; $\frac{5}{10} = \frac{50}{100}$

Problem Solving

1. Grade 1; $\frac{6}{10} = \frac{60}{100}$; $\frac{60}{100} > \frac{34}{100}$; $\frac{6}{10} > \frac{3}{10}$; $\frac{60}{100} > \frac{52}{100}$
2. Grade 3; $\frac{3}{10} = \frac{30}{100}$; $\frac{3}{10} < \frac{6}{10}$; $\frac{30}{100} < \frac{34}{100}$; $\frac{30}{100} < \frac{52}{100}$
3. $\frac{94}{100}$; $\frac{6}{10} = \frac{60}{100}$; $\frac{60}{100} + \frac{34}{100} = \frac{94}{100}$
4. $\frac{82}{100}$; $\frac{3}{10} = \frac{30}{100}$; $\frac{30}{100} + \frac{52}{100} = \frac{82}{100}$
5. Grades 1 and 2; Explanations will vary but should include that $\frac{94}{100} > \frac{82}{100}$.